One Village Makes a Difference

Rob Waring, *Series Editor*

HEINLE
CENGAGE Learning

Australia · Canada · Mexico · Singapore · United Kingdom · United States

Words to Know

This story is set in India. It happens in the city of New Delhi [dɛli], and in the Alwar [ʌlwər] region of the state of Rajasthan [rɑdʒəstɑn].

A **Water Words.** Read the paragraph. Then match each word with the correct definition.

People everywhere need many gallons of water a day for drinking, washing, and other activities. People also use water to irrigate dry land so that they can grow food on it. How can people get this water in dry, desert areas? One way is to build a dam across a river. This stops the flow of water and dries up the river bed. These dams create reservoirs that hold water until people use it. Another way to get water is to collect it from wells that go deep into the earth.

1. gallon _____

2. irrigate _____

3. desert _____

4. dam _____

5. river bed _____

6. reservoir _____

7. well _____

a. a place for storing water for later use

b. a wall built across a river to stop the river's flow

c. a measurement used for water (3.78 liters)

d. supply land with water for growing plants

e. a region that has very little water

f. the area of land where a river flows

g. a deep hole in the ground from which water is collected

reservoir

B India's Water Problem. Complete the paragraph with the words in the box.

conserve	invested	shortage
environmentalist	rupees*	

From its large cities to its small villages, India has a big problem: a (1)_____ of water. People have (2)_____ a lot of money to get fresh water to the population. They have spent millions of (3)_____ on large dams and other projects. Rajendra Singh [rɑdʒɑndrə sɪnhə] is an (4)_____ who knows about the earth and its systems. He says that these methods won't work. Instead, he's teaching one region to use an ancient method to save, or (5)_____, water. The method seems to be working because there's now enough water in the area.

* $1 U.S. = about 40 rupees

desert

well

dam

river bed

New Delhi is a very large city in northern India. It has a large population and, like any big city, it faces a number of challenging problems. The heavy **smog**[1] that usually covers the area is so unclean that it's difficult to see the city. Unfortunately, New Delhi's water supply doesn't look much better.

New Delhi is situated on the Yamuna River, which is the main **source**[2] of drinking water for the people of the city. Fifty million gallons of industrial waste are thrown into the Yamuna River every single day. This sometimes makes the city's main water supply look more like a science experiment than a water source.

---

[1]**smog:** thick, dirty air in a city
[2]**source:** the place where something comes from

 CD 2, Track 01

Predict

Answer 'True' or 'False'. Then, scan page 6 to check your answers.

1. Forty million people live in New Delhi.

2. The people there need one billion gallons of water a day.

3. They are now living on 25 percent of that, or 250 million gallons a day.

4. Only the poorer people are experiencing a water shortage.

Because of the terrible condition of the river, the 14 million people in and around New Delhi must get their water from community water trucks. These trucks deliver water to the towns where people live. Sometimes people must wait for the water trucks to arrive, even when they are very thirsty. Sometimes there's enough water for everyone, and sometimes there isn't.

The people of New Delhi need about one billion gallons of water every day. At the moment, they are surviving on only 25 percent of that, or 250 million gallons. The water shortage is not limited to only the poorer parts of the city, either. In the richer areas of New Delhi, you'll find busy shopping centers, well-dressed shoppers, and expensive restaurants. You can also find the same community water trucks.

People must often wait for community water trucks to arrive.

Farther outside of the city, in the desert of Rajasthan, getting water is even harder. The temperatures frequently reach as high as **120 degrees Fahrenheit**.[3] Villagers must walk for **miles**[4] to get water. Then, when they finally reach a well, they often have to drink next to their animals.

Every year in India and other southern Asian countries there's a season of heavy rain. This is called the monsoon season. The annual monsoon rains do bring water, but these rains only provide relief for a short time. They don't replace the amount of water that's used every year. So the same question remains: Is there an answer to India's water problem?

---

[3]**120 degrees Fahrenheit:** 48.89 degrees Celsius
[4]**mile:** 1 mile = 1.6 kilometers

Some leaders seem to think that the answer lies in a series of new dams. However, many people strongly disagree with this proposal. These people believe that India's existing dams have contributed to the water shortage. They say that the dams dry up the river beds, fields, and wells.

One environmentalist, Rajendra Singh, feels strongly about the dam issue. "Thousands of millions of rupees have already been invested in water policy and big dams. How do you explain villages with no water?" he asks. "Who is responsible for all this?" he says, and then answers his own question. "Well, the **blame**[5] lies on the very system which **advocates**[6] the construction of bigger dams," Singh explains. For Singh, building dams doesn't seem to be the answer to the water problem. Where can India find it?

---

[5]**blame:** say or think that someone or something caused a problem
[6]**advocate:** express support for something

The answer to India's water shortage may be found in a group of villages in the Alwar area of Rajasthan. In this region, Singh has started a **non-governmental organization**[7] that works with villagers to make clean water easily available.

Singh encourages villagers to use an ancient method to collect more water for the area. The method uses small dams to help store water and to greatly change the land. Under Singh's direction, the people in a village in Alwar decided to try the method. They wanted to see if it would work.

---

[7]**non-governmental organization (NGO):** an organization that is independent of government, business, etc.

The process began with villagers collecting stone and rock to make small **earthen**[8] dams. The villagers then made small pits, or holes, near them. They laid a **porous**[9] layer of stone, earth, and **clay**[10] in the holes. The stone, earth, and clay stopped the rain water from running off of the land. The dams and pits created a source of water that lasted longer than the monsoons. They also raised the level of the water under the ground. With every rain shower, this ground water level rose higher. Eventually, people were able to create wells to irrigate their farms. Soon, water reached every part of the village!

---

[8]**earthen:** made of earth or dirt
[9]**porous:** with many small holes; allowing water to pass through
[10]**clay:** thick, heavy earth that is soft when wet, and hard when dry

wet well

Earthen dams actually raised the ground water levels in Alwar!

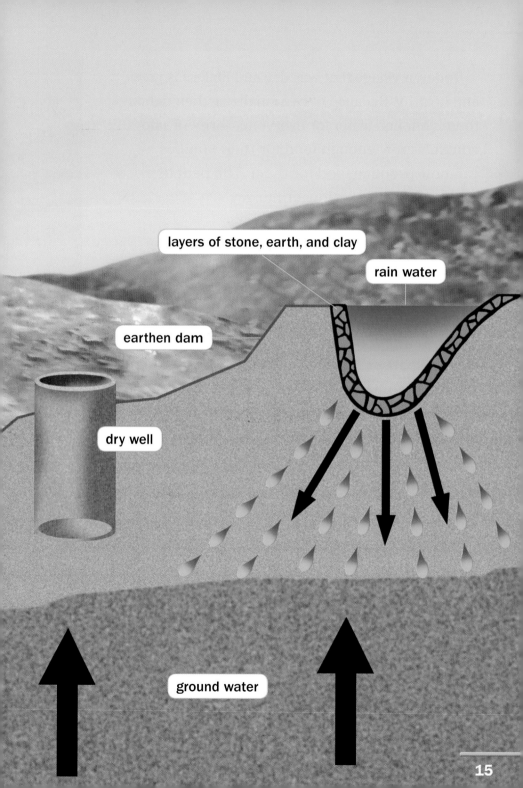

layers of stone, earth, and clay

rain water

earthen dam

dry well

ground water

15

Today, a village that was dry and lifeless is green and healthy. Because of two small, earthen dams, there's enough water for everyone. Farmers who couldn't grow enough food for their families can now produce food for them. The people of the village are no longer hungry.

Now, other villages are learning how to make these dams. One man explains how his village is learning from a neighboring village. "We're building water reservoirs and dams to save rain water. We want our village, Rosda, to be green and **prosperous**[11] like Neemie," he says. At present, there are more than 4,000 earthen dams collecting rain water across western India. These dams, made with ancient methods, provide water for more than 800 communities. This water conservation strategy is certainly a success story for the villages of Alwar. What about New Delhi?

----

[11]**prosperous:** rich; doing well economically

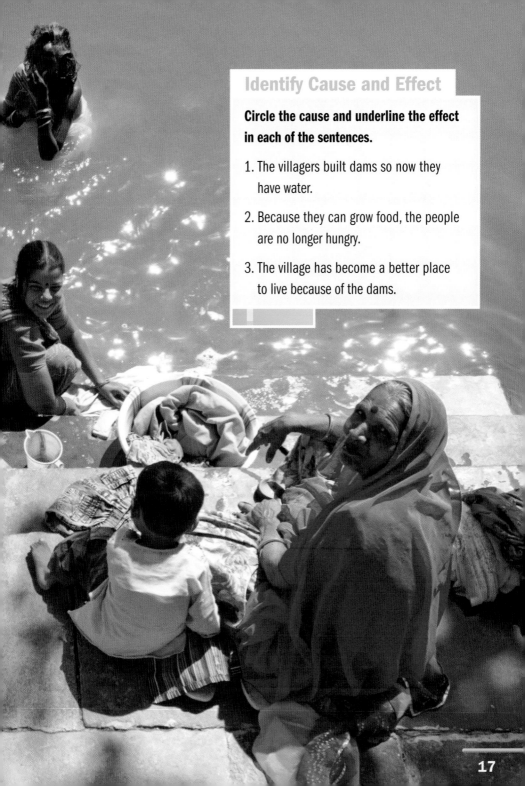

Identify Cause and Effect

Circle the cause and underline the effect in each of the sentences.

1. The villagers built dams so now they have water.

2. Because they can grow food, the people are no longer hungry.

3. The village has become a better place to live because of the dams.

17

The small scale conservation methods that people are using in Alwar are not practical for New Delhi. They would not be enough to help such a big city. Experts say that new water supplies and efforts to conserve water may slow the water shortage there, but only for a short time. They predict that the problem would return in ten years time.

Perhaps the big cities can learn something from Alwar. Certainly, things have changed for the better there. These days, the people of Alwar no longer have to walk a long way to look for water. A well full of water is just down the road. It seems that in the region of Alwar, one village really can make a difference!

After You Read

1. Because of smog, New Delhi can almost _____ be seen.
   A. always
   B. never
   C. occasionally
   D. totally

2. On page 4, the writer gives details about the smog to:
   A. show that it's New Delhi's only problem
   B. explain that the air is worse than the water
   C. introduce a similar problem with water
   D. show that the city's population is large

3. Which is a suitable heading for page 6?
   A. Both Rich and Poor Need Water Trucks
   B. Trucks Have Plenty of Water
   C. Thirsty People Drive Trucks
   D. Forty Million People Wait for Water

4. Which of the following is NOT a problem for villagers in Rajasthan?
   A. hot weather
   B. animals
   C. well locations
   D. no monsoon rains

5. In paragraph 1 on page 11, 'they' refers to people who:
   A. lead India
   B. disagree with the dam proposal
   C. make the dams
   D. invest rupees

6. What view is expressed by Rajendra Singh on page 11?
   A. Villagers are responsible for the problem.
   B. Bigger dams will fix the problem.
   C. The current system is not working.
   D. The water policy supports the people.

7. In paragraph 1 on page 13, the phrase, 'be found in'
can be replaced by:
  A. work with
  B. reply to
  C. end with
  D. come from

8. Match the correct cause to the effect.
Effect: Rain water is stopped from running off.
  A. Villagers make small holes in the earth.
  B. Villagers make a new source of water.
  C. Villagers put stone, earth, and clay in a hole.
  D. Villagers have water in every part of the area.

9. In paragraph 2 on page 16, the phrase 'at present' means:
  A. now
  B. before
  C. then
  D. later

10. Which is a good heading for page 16?
  A. Neemie Learns from Rosda
  B. Villagers Teach Each Other
  C. Four Hundred Earth Dams
  D. Modern Methods Are Successful

11. The water-collecting method used in Alwar will NOT help
New Delhi because:
  A. There is not enough earth there.
  B. The people there won't try it.
  C. The smog problem is more important.
  D. The population is too large.

12. What is the writer's opinion on page 19?
  A. Big cities may be able to learn from small villages.
  B. New Delhi can reach success in ten years.
  C. Small-scale water systems can be used everywhere.
  D. The city's water shortage can be solved.

The Hoover Dam

The Hoover Dam was constructed for a number of reasons. U.S. President Herbert Hoover played a major role in its planning and development. He wanted to build a dam on the Colorado River to produce electricity. Like many of today's world leaders, Hoover understood the importance of making more electricity. He also wanted to stop the river from destroying nearby towns when the water levels became too high. He and his team of researchers suggested closing the river in a place called Boulder Canyon to create a large lake. It took almost 13 years, and a lot of hard work, to create the dam at Boulder Canyon. However, the benefits of the project were well worth it.

Colorado River Controlled

For years, the Colorado River regularly damaged the areas around it in times of heavy rain. In 1905, the Colorado River flowed out of its bed and completely covered a 388 square kilometer* area. The area remained covered with water for nearly two years and became known as the Salton Sea. After that, environmentalists and safety advocates wanted to protect the area and control the powerful river. Since the dam was built, there have been no more problems around Boulder Canyon due to the river flowing out of its bed.

The Hoover Dam

*See page 24 for a metric conversion chart.

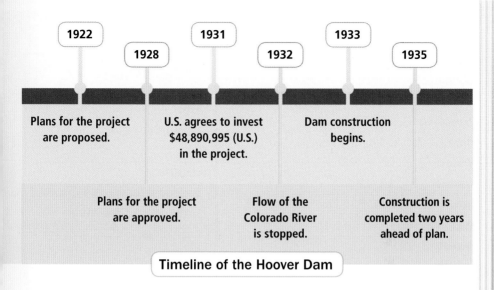

1922	1928	1931	1932	1933	1935

Plans for the project are proposed.

Plans for the project are approved.

U.S. agrees to invest $48,890,995 (U.S.) in the project.

Flow of the Colorado River is stopped.

Dam construction begins.

Construction is completed two years ahead of plan.

Timeline of the Hoover Dam

Irrigation Provided

At the time, there was a lot of rich farmland around the Colorado River. However, there was not a dependable water source available, so farmers could not make the land productive. Upon its completion, the dam provided a regular water supply. It now provides for the irrigation of more than 6,000 square kilometers of land in California, Arizona, and the country of Mexico. These irrigated lands supply large amounts of produce and other farm products to the world market.

A Major Power Source Created

The Hoover Dam has become one of the world's largest suppliers of electric power. It now produces enough energy annually to supply 1.3 million people with electricity. The power created at the Hoover Dam provides energy to the states of California, Arizona and Nevada. The estimated percentage of power delivered to each state is: Arizona, 19 percent; Nevada, 23.4 percent; and California, 57.6 percent.

CD 2, Track 02

Word Count: 347
Time: _____

Vocabulary List

advocate (11)
blame (11)
clay (14, 15)
conserve (3, 16, 19)
dam (2, 3, 11, 13, 14, 15, 16, 17)
desert (2, 3, 9)
earthen (14, 15, 16)
environmentalist (3, 11)
gallon (2, 4, 5, 6)
invest (3, 11)
irrigate (2, 14)
mile (9)
non-governmental organization (NGO) (13)
porous (14)
prosperous (16)
reservoir (2, 16)
river bed (2, 3, 11)
rupee (3, 11)
shortage (3, 5, 6, 11, 13, 19)
smog (4)
source (4, 14)
well (2, 3, 9, 11, 14, 15, 19)

Metric Conversion Chart

Area
1 hectare = 2.471 acres

Length
1 centimeter = .394 inches
1 meter = 1.094 yards
1 kilometer = .621 miles

Temperature
0° Celsius = 32° Fahrenheit

Volume
1 liter = 1.057 quarts

Weight
1 gram = .035 ounces
1 kilogram = 2.2 pounds